KINGDOM IN YOUR MIDST

I0221716

KINGDOM IN YOUR MIDST

The Message Behind the Preaching of Jesus

By
ROBERT F. SCHUT

RESOURCE *Publications* · Eugene, Oregon

KINGDOM IN YOUR MIDST
The Message Behind the Preaching of Jesus

Copyright © 2015 Robert F. Schut. All rights reserved. Except for brief
quotations in critical publications or reviews, no part of this book may
be reproduced in any manner without prior written permission from the
publisher. Write: Permissions, Wipf and Stock Publishers, 199 W. 8th Ave.,
Suite 3, Eugene, OR 97401.

Resource Publications
An Imprint of Wipf and Stock Publishers
199 W. 8th Ave., Suite 3
Eugene, OR 97401

www.wipfandstock.com

ISBN 13: 978-1-4982-2054-5

Manufactured in the U.S.A.   02/12/2015

Scripture and/or notes quoted by permission. Quotations designated
(NET) are from the NET Bible® copyright ©1996–2006 by Biblical Studies
Press, L.L.C. All rights reserved.

Scripture quotations marked KJV are taken from the King James Version
of the Bible.

To my wife Diane, my daughters,
and my grandchildren with love.

Contents

Preface

I BEGAN THIS BOOK thinking how difficult it might be for me to fill up a whole book written only on the kingdom of heaven since it seemed like a narrow topic and there's really not a lot of books written specifically on this subject to use as references. But I soon began to realize how much scripture has to say about the kingdom, albeit cloaked in elements such as the law, prophecy, and parables. I then began to doubt how I could possibly fit all the mysteries and wonder of such a kingdom into only one book and still maintain control over such a massive task with my limited skill as a writer.

This book is an accumulation of many years spent gathering information on each included topic, such as: the law, the church, the parables, etc. There is certainly a value to each element as it stands on its own, but we cannot neglect the dynamics created when we are able to link them all together and see them as having one common goal or purpose. It is somewhat like putting the pieces of a puzzle together where each one not only joins but supports the other pieces creating a more holistic picture than is seen in the individual pieces.

The result is a book shorter than most as far as quantity of pages, but hopefully deeper than most in that it might inspire the reader to see these elements in a new way that will bring the kingdom into a clearer perspective where he can fit the final piece into the picture—himself.

This book certainly does not contain everything there is to know about the kingdom of heaven. My approach to writing this book can be summed up as "less is more." Perhaps it will confirm what you already have been wondering about the kingdom; or it may begin a whole new journey in your Christian life. My deepest hope is that it changes your life and brings you closer to God as well as to your fellow believer.

This book is not meant to be a source of knowledge, but rather a finger pointing to something much greater. It is meant to point you back to the basic message that Christ taught to his disciples which is one of many threads that runs through the writings of the New Testament authors.

On the question of pronoun gender as used in this book I chose to present the neutral gender as masculine only as a matter of convenience and literary flow. There is nothing to be presumed by the reader concerning my choice of masculine over feminine where gender is neutral.

Abbreviations

NET   New English Bible Translation

KJV   King James Bible Translation

BDAG   Walter Bauer, Frederick W. Danker, W. F. Arndt, and F. W. Gingrich. *Greek-English Lexicon of the New Testament and Other Early Christian Literature.* 3rd ed. Chicago: University of Chicago Press, 2000.

Matthew 7:7–8 (KJV)

Ask, and it shall be given you; seek, and ye shall find;
knock, and it shall be opened unto you:
For every one that asketh receiveth; and he that seeketh findeth;
and to him that knocketh it shall be opened.

1

Introduction

As a Bible teacher I find it an ongoing challenge to take stories, letters, and sayings from the Bible and present them with interesting insights into their meaning. I have to check authorities, commentaries, and even consider the original languages in order to validate old as well as justify new ideas to be discussed. One of the most difficult challenges, however, is to take scripture meant for the first-century Jewish culture and make it applicable for today's generation.

Perhaps one of the most difficult topics to make relevant today is Jesus' teachings on the kingdom of heaven, which is also referred to as the kingdom of God. It is this topic that I wish to address in this small, but hopefully concise book.

Why is the kingdom of heaven so mysterious that Jesus would only speak of it in parables? Is it something that is so beyond the average person's understanding that only saints, gurus, or mystics can understand it?

Perhaps it is because the kingdom of heaven addresses our deepest sense of who we are. But it is not just the sense of self of which Jesus is speaking; it is the relationship of that self as it comes to know God in a very special and unique way. He describes the way that we will begin to see ourselves, others, and God as we live in God's kingdom where this self takes on a whole new value based upon God's system and not our own.

Jesus spoke about the kingdom of heaven more as a reign of power than as a place.[1] He also spoke about how this will affect the way we perceive ourselves and others now that we are under this new rule and protection of God's lordship. This new evaluation is often the complete opposite of what we might expect in our present-day world. Many of our values today are turned upside-down. Those things which we consider to be of greatest importance are really of least importance in God's kingdom. It is for this reason that many of us may feel a sense of conflict between our faith and our everyday lives.

In our world the poor, persecuted, and mournful are considered to be those who have been cursed by God—but in his kingdom these very same people are actually the blessed!

Although Jesus was a teacher, he was not explaining what the kingdom was from the point of view of a philosopher or a theologian. He was teaching it from the viewpoint of one who lives every moment in this kingdom. He tries to give us a sense of what he experienced through situations experienced in everyday life which create in us and in his audience the same sense of wonder and awe that are created in God's kingdom—perhaps though on a smaller scale.

The point of Jesus' parables was not to entertain us with little stories or create some poetic imagery from which to compose elaborate interpretations. He told these stories to make us aware that there was a whole other worldliness higher and greater than this one where God ruled over everything and everyone. It was not simply a pie-in-the-sky vision of some fantasy place or even a place that might someday exist in the future. It is a place that exists here and now—in their midst as well as ours. It is the experience of having the right attitude towards God which all people can potentially have, though many have failed to realize and exhibit.

Jesus' declaration is that such a kingdom has already come upon us. It has come upon us in the form of a man who would

1. Blomberg, *Jesus and the Gospels*, 384.

show us the way not by merely talking about it, but by becoming it. If we walk as he walked, we too will experience the awe and wonder of this kingdom of God.[2]

One enters into such a kingdom, not only through the confession of God's almighty power, but by recognizing and seeking after God's righteousness as displayed in and by Jesus, his Christ. Therefore, we must always keep in mind that God's kingdom is not only a kingdom of power and glory, but also one of righteousness.

What then does the kingdom of God mean to us today? Is Jesus' teaching really relevant to us in modern times? I believe the answer is "Yes," but we must seek out his kingdom as it presents itself to us in our reality today. The kingdom of God still exists today just as it did in the first century. We simply have to look for it in the events that surround *our* existence. But we must not only *seek* it out, we must also *live* it out with the intent upon it becoming our ultimate true reality. We must make treasures for ourselves now that will last for eternity, and by doing so we will reassure ourselves of our place in this kingdom.

Now some might think that this is all just another idea enabling Christians to escape from the real world and its problems, but rather it is God's way of engaging the real world, his world, with a new sense of hope and confidence. Today, too many Christians feel overwhelmed by their problems and feel hopeless and even worthless as they struggle through those problems. The kingdom of God brings to us a new vision of those problems as well as a way to overcome those self-defeating thoughts that accompany such problems.

According to Leon Morris "the kingdom is the most important topic in Jesus' teaching."[3] And Seyoon Kim claims that the kingdom of God is "the central theme of Jesus' preaching."[4] The

2. 1 John 2:5–6.

3. Morris, *The Gospel According to Matthew*, 53. Although Morris limits this precedence to Matthew, Mark, and Luke (the Synoptics); John's gospel also makes great importance of the kingdom message, but gives precedence to the divine identity of Christ.

4. Kim, *The Son of Man*, 76.

kingdom of God gives us a world-view that God has created for those who believe in his Son. It gives us a new perspective of who we are and a sense of self-worth not only as believers, but as sons and daughters of God.

Now the kingdom of heaven is different than most other subjects. Most of the books that I have in my library contain a lot of facts backed by other facts and so on. In some books the footnotes take up more room than the text. For certain subjects this is really the best and maybe the only way for the author to present his opinions. Although this works for many subjects, I think that it is a mistake to try to present the kingdom of heaven using this same format.

The kingdom of heaven is unique and presenting it to the reader by overwhelming him with historical and theological facts may not be the best approach. It certainly was not Jesus' approach, in that he particularly chose stories or parables by which to communicate it.

Stories such as parables tend to engage the reader or listener in the process of truth as he is confronted face to face with his own ideas and prejudices. This was the power of the parable in the hands of Jesus. He led his listeners to the point of truth by exposing their true feelings through their own response. This is the beginning of truth no matter how stark and sobering it might be.

In the same manner, though much less prophetic, I will try to engage you as the reader in a dialogue as we both seek towards the truth together. It is my hope that the following chapters bring greater clarity to your vision of God's kingdom and inspire many to seek it out with a passion that will take them into a deeper relationship with God than they ever thought possible.

DISCUSSION QUESTIONS

1. What is your current understanding of the kingdom of heaven?

2. Why do you think Jesus used parables about the kingdom rather than plainly tell his disciples what the kingdom was?

3. Do you think it's possible to live in Jesus' kingdom in today's world?

4. What things seem different in God's kingdom than in man's kingdom?

5. Do you consider trials and tribulations in your life to be curses or blessings? (Be honest now)

6. How do you seek the kingdom of heaven today?

7. How can this new vision of the kingdom help us live out our faith?

NOTES

Luke 17:20–21 (NET)

Now at one point the Pharisees asked Jesus when the kingdom of God was coming, so he answered, "The kingdom of God is not coming with signs to be observed, nor will they say, 'Look, here it is!' or 'There!' For indeed, the kingdom of God is in your midst."

2

Where Is the Kingdom?

I THINK THAT MANY people would answer this question by quoting Jesus in Luke 17:21 (KJV) when he said that the kingdom of heaven is *within* you, but this is actually an awkward rendering of the Greek text. What Jesus probably said was that the kingdom of God is *among you, near you, within your grasp,* or *in your midst.*[1] Although it is true that we experience the kingdom in our hearts and that we all have the potential to enter it, the context here was not of some Buddhist type of Nirvana or a remnant spark of divinity that *already* lies within each of us, but that Jesus himself was the point of entry into the kingdom. He was the only, truly-anointed king that had the authority to rule in it.

In other words, we must first accept him as the true king if we want to live in his kingdom. C.E.B. Cranfield expresses this idea very well saying that the kingdom of heaven is intimately connected with Jesus himself, and it is this intimacy that has come upon them. "[I]t is because he [Jesus] is in their midst that it [the kingdom] is in their midst."[2]

---

1. NET, Luke 21, Note 65. BDAG, 340. Blomberg, *Jesus and the Gospels,* 293.

2. Cranfield, *The Gospel According to St Mark,* 66.

Jesus proclaimed his kingdom in this way all throughout his ministry. Other verses that he used to convey this idea are:

> But if I cast out devils by the Spirit of God, then the kingdom of God is come unto you. (Matt 12:28 KJV)

> Now after that John was put in prison, Jesus came into Galilee, preaching the gospel of the kingdom of God, And saying, The time is fulfilled, and the kingdom of God is at hand: repent ye, and believe the gospel. (Mark 1:14–15 KJV)

> Heal the sick in that town and say to them, 'The kingdom of God has come upon you!' (Luke 10:9 NET)

As you can read from the above verses, Jesus is, without a doubt, linked to the coming of God's kingdom. It was not *within* them, but *in their midst*.

This does not mean that there is no internal experience or feelings that accompany the kingdom for there surely are, but these feelings are responses and effects of the presence of the kingdom and not the kingdom itself. The kingdom *itself* is found only in the presence of God in Christ.

Jesus didn't teach his kingdom as some ideological kingdom far, far, away. Rather, he brought his kingdom upon us through his cross which pierced through our reality and into his, enabling man not only to *seek* after God's kingdom, but to actually *enter* into it for all eternity.[3]

Unfortunately, many today make the mistake of thinking of the kingdom of heaven as a place where they can enter into only after they die. It's a kind of fantasyland where the good people go to live out their eternal lives in utter happiness and joy, but has no real connection to the living. I guess we can partially thank Hollywood for that version. Unfortunately, no one has really done much to alter that perception.

Perhaps the reason this idea is so popular is because people do not bother to make a connection between heaven and their own reality, yet this was the whole intent of Jesus' teaching on the

---

3. Bruce, *Paul Apostle of the Heart Set Free*, 97.

kingdom. He preached that the kingdom had come upon them and is right now in their midst. He confronted not only the beggars, vendors, and street people that came to listen to him, but the priests and Pharisees who came to spy upon him as well—and all had an opportunity to enter.

The kingdom of God is neither limited by location or time. It exists in Jerusalem, Rome, England, and the USA. It existed during the time of Christ, Paul, and Luther and still exists today.

It isn't limited by time since it is eternal in the sense that God is and was always King, but his eternal kingdom was not always realized by man. It wasn't until Christ came and announced it through word and deed that it became more fully revealed to us. And it was through the resurrection that Jesus was not only proclaimed, but was also inaugurated as king over all the earth. It was at that time that man could once again become an eternal member of God's kingdom having been forgiven and restored by grace.

If you are still having a little trouble understanding the kingdom and our relationship to it, consider the conversation between Jesus and Nicodemus in the Gospel of John chapter 3.

> *Jesus answered and said unto him, Verily, verily, I say unto thee, Except a man be born again, he cannot see the kingdom of God. (John 3:3 KJV)*

Although the phrase is often misused or at least overused, the idea of being born again in the original context of the kingdom of heaven was that it meant seeing one's reality from an entirely new spiritual relationship with God. It is a spiritual awakening concerning not simply the truth as some ideology or doctrine, but truth as a living relationship between man and God. It is a way of life, an engagement with the truth, not simply a new idea or philosophy. To put it simply, *the kingdom of heaven is the spiritual bond that we have with God through Christ.* To quote Paul, "If anyone is in Christ, he is a new creation, the old has passed away; behold, the new has come."[4] It is in this new bond where we

4. 2 Cor 5:17.

will find the kingdom. It is a bond not cemented by law, ritual, or philosophy, but by faith and trust.

As we will see in a later chapter, Jesus did not speak directly to the kingdom as though it were a physical place, but used symbolic ideas and parables to convey its meaning. If we are looking for a roadmap to the kingdom or a twelve-step program that will lead us there, we will be sorely disappointed. What we can do is simply *listen* to the call of God through the words of Christ, submit to it and seek after it.

If the kingdom is within our grasp and in our midst, why then do men have such a difficult time finding it?

The short answer is that we are simply too busy creating our own kingdoms. These can be kingdoms of wealth, power, or even ideology. Jesus called such kingdoms houses built upon sand because they are not only temporary, but they are easily brought to destruction.

> And every one that heareth these sayings of mine, and doeth them not, shall be likened unto a foolish man, which built his house upon the sand: And the rain descended, and the floods came, and the winds blew, and beat upon that house; and it fell: and great was the fall of it. (Matt 7:26–27 KJV)

The reason that we choose to build our own kingdoms instead of accepting God's probably varies with each individual, but I think that fear plays a major role. Man fears not being in control of his own destiny. Power, wealth, and even ideas can bring about a false sense of confidence and certainty that enable man to feel that he has in some way retained control over his fate. As long as he can maintain his own self-worth through these methods, he is able to preserve a sense of certainty about himself. Jesus and his kingdom merely become another ideology that he can either assimilate or accommodate into his own, where he still remains king. We will speak more on this issue in other chapters.

Now before we move on to the next chapter I think I need to address the question of whether the kingdom of God and the kingdom of heaven are the same thing.

A common belief held by theologians is that during the time of Jesus the Jews avoided saying the name of God for fear of committing blasphemy, which was a capital offense. It is for this reason that Matthew, being a Jew, frequently substituted the word *heaven* for *God*. The expressions kingdom of God and kingdom of heaven are identical.[5] One need only compare the sayings of Jesus between Matthew and the other gospels to find support for this conclusion. Throughout this book I have followed the convention that both references refer to the same thing.

5. For more on this subject see Morris, *The Gospel According to Matthew,* 8, 53; Cranfield, *The Gospel According to St Mark,* 64; Blomberg, *Jesus and the Gospels, 233, 387.*

DISCUSSION QUESTIONS

1. Do you agree with C.E.B. Cranfield's quotation about Christ being in our midst?

2. What is the difference between the kingdom of heaven being within you as opposed to being in your midst?

3. What is the underlying theme that Jesus preaches in the scriptures quoted (Matt 12:28, Mark 1:14–15, Luke 10:9)?

4. If Jesus's kingdom had truly come upon those to whom he preached in the first century, what impact should that have had upon their lives? What impact should it have upon our lives today?

5. Can you think of any movies that have influenced our thinking about heaven? Explain.

6. Is it important that we differentiate between actually being in the kingdom and the feelings that might accompany it? What are the consequences if we don't?

7. What does the kingdom mean in the context of the verse *to be born again*?

8. So where is the kingdom of heaven?

NOTES

Matthew 13:31–32 (NET)

He gave them another parable: "The kingdom of heaven is like a mustard seed that a man took and sowed in his field. It is the smallest of all the seeds, but when it has grown it is the greatest garden plant and becomes a tree, so that the wild birds come and nest in its branches."

3

What Is the Kingdom Like?

JESUS GAVE US NUMEROUS parables to try to explain what the kingdom was like. These parables were meant to give us a sense of both attitude and experience that might be similar to what we would have in the kingdom of heaven, though on a smaller scale. The idea was that these were but samples of a heavenly experience.

Many of these parables give us the sense that God's kingdom must be considered more valuable than anything else in our lives. It must become our primary concern and goal.

So, in essence, it is a state of existence where we no longer place ourselves at the center of importance, but place God there instead. It is at this moment that we see God as our ultimate truth and begin to experience his kingdom under his undisputed lordship. It is at this point that we realize the true value of our relationship with God and the failure of all other attempts to create such a relationship as mere imitation.

There are many parables that Jesus used to describe and explain the many facets of the kingdom of heaven, and if I went over all of them, this would turn into a book about parables rather than the kingdom. So I will use only a few to explain the particular points about seeking the kingdom that I wish to make here. These parables that explicitly speak about the kingdom of heaven are referred to as so-called "kingdom parables."[1]

The kingdom is like a found treasure:

> *The kingdom of heaven is like a treasure, hidden in a field, that a person found and hid. Then because of joy he went and sold all that he had and bought that field. (Matt 13:44 NET)*

The basic idea behind this parable is that we should do whatever it takes and make any sacrifice in order to obtain the kingdom since we recognize that it is a treasure far more valuable than anything we currently own.

> *He gave them another parable: "The kingdom of heaven is like a mustard seed that a man took and sowed in his field. It is the smallest of all the seeds, but when it has grown it is the greatest garden plant and becomes a tree, so that the wild birds come and nest in its branches. (Matt 13:31–32 NET)"*

There are many complex interpretations of this parable, but at its root is the idea that God's kingdom does not operate on the same value or logical system as our own. It is a parable that teaches us through contrast. One would expect the size of a plant to be directly proportional to the size of the seed, but this example teaches us that such preconceived notions aren't always true. It is upon such false ideas and preconceptions that we sometimes base our ideas of God's kingdom. What we consider to be almost insignificant in our value system may be seen as having great potential in God's kingdom.

Cranfield also suggests that this parable relates to the unassuming and insignificant beginning of the kingdom as compared to its glorious fulfillment.[2]

---

1. Conner, *Mystery Parables*, *18*. See the first 6 chapters for some good insight into the study of parables.

2. Cranfield, *The Gospel According to St Mark*, *170*.

> *He told them another parable: "The kingdom of heaven is*
> *like yeast that a woman took and mixed with three mea-*
> *sures of flour until all the dough had risen." (Matt 13:33*
> *NET)*

Here again is a parable that has interpretations that cover a wide and even contradictory scope of meanings, but the basic impression we get here is that the effects of the kingdom of heaven are mysterious and can sometimes only be recognized by the end result or effect. It is something that works mysteriously within us and shows its effects outwardly.

> *Again, the kingdom of heaven is like unto a merchant man,*
> *seeking goodly pearls: Who, when he had found one pearl*
> *of great price, went and sold all that he had, and bought it.*
> *(Matthew 13:45–46 KJV)*

Again we have a parable that expresses the idea of finding something that is more valuable than anything else like it. The response is to do whatever it takes to possess it. Notice that Jesus uses symbols that were appropriate to his first-century audience. Each culture may place different values on objects, but the fact remains that appealing to man's desire for wealth is always a safe bet.

> *"Again, the kingdom of heaven is like a net that was cast*
> *into the sea that caught all kinds of fish. When it was full,*
> *they pulled it ashore, sat down, and put the good fish into*
> *containers and threw the bad away. It will be this way at*
> *the end of the age. Angels will come and separate the evil*
> *from the righteous. . . ."(Matthew 13:47–49 NET)*

I would be remiss if I didn't include this parable even though it might not sound politically correct to our sensitive ears. It is nevertheless part of Jesus' teaching of the kingdom and, therefore it should be included here.

Although there are a lot of ways to twist and turn this parable to make it say some very interesting things, I think it best to keep it as simple as possible here.

As the message of the kingdom goes out into the world, it is heard by many. However, not all will respond in the same way. Those who respond positively to it will be considered the righteous ones, while those who do not, will be considered the evil ones. The good or righteous ones will be saved, while the bad or evil ones will be thrown away.

The message is pretty simple. The deciding factor in how you spend eternity is based upon your reaction to the kingdom message. There are many other teachings one might pull out of this parable, but the basic message does not change—hear the gospel and believe it or suffer the consequences.

We will see in the following chapters exactly what the correct response might be, but for now I think I have made my point.

There are many more parables that could be used to demonstrate these ideas, but once you know what to look for you can search through them on your own with little help from anyone.[3]

But so far I have not really explained what the kingdom itself is like, why it's a treasure, and what makes it so valuable that we would want to sell all we have to obtain it. No one chapter will answer all these questions about the kingdom as it will be more a sum total of understanding from all the chapters. Some answers can only be obtained from your own particular experience in the kingdom, but please read on for more on this topic.

---

3. For further information I recommend reading several books on parables as they will differ greatly in their interpretation. See list of titles under Recommended Reading for Further Study at the end of this book.

DISCUSSION QUESTIONS

1. What is the most valuable thing in your life?

2. At this moment what would you consider the purpose of your life?

3. Have you had any failed attempts in your relationship with God? Why did they fail?

4. Do you think that parables address the kingdom of heaven as something we have or something we seek? What is the effect of this?

5. Can you give an example of something that fits the same contrasting idea of a mustard seed?

6. If you have alternative meanings to the parables listed here, evaluate those meanings with your own experience of the kingdom.

7. How would you explain exactly *what* the kingdom of heaven is?

NOTES

Matthew 10:7 (KJV)

And as ye go, preach, saying, 'The kingdom of heaven is at hand.'

4

When Will the Kingdom Come?

As we stated earlier, the kingdom is already here. It is now in the process of being revealed more fully until the day of Christ's coming when its fullness will become complete and evident to all.

So the kingdom is already here in the sense that we may enter it now and for all eternity. It is already here in the sense that we can realize the kingship of Christ over this world and its evil. It is already here in the sense that we have been given power over sin and the powers of this world.[1]

But it is not fully and completely here in that we are still clothed with bodies that are more suited to this world than the world to come. So we must make do with what we have. These are the bodies that Paul encourages us to offer to God as a living sacrifice:

> *I beseech you therefore, brethren, by the mercies of God, that ye present your bodies a living sacrifice, holy, acceptable unto God, which is your reasonable service. (Rom 12:1 KJV)*

---

1. 1 John 2:12–14.

KINGDOM IN YOUR MIDST

We can realize its presence here and now, but must also look forward to the fullness of its coming when Jesus returns as King, Savior, and Judge.

We must not take lightly our entreaty to God in the Lord's Prayer when we pray asking in a sober mind to let his kingdom come. Neither should we pray to God as Saint Augustine did asking, "Lord make me pure—but not yet!"[2] Let us not pray with such a double-mindedness, but ask as though our prayer will in itself bring about the coming of the kingdom.

In the same manner that we anticipate having a perfect body in the kingdom of heaven we must also anticipate having the perfect spirit. Although we must wait for the Day of the Lord when we put on our perfect bodies, we can begin to put on the perfect spirit here and now.

It is with this same attitude that we seek to clothe ourselves in perfect, eternal bodies that we should have in clothing ourselves in the perfect, eternal spirit. It is in this same attitude that we take confidence in our faith and its power over sin.

> And now, little children, abide in him; that, when he shall appear, we may have confidence, and not be ashamed before him at his coming. If ye know that he is righteous, ye know that every one that doeth righteousness is born of him. (1 John 2:28–29 KJV)

Now you might be wondering how the kingdom fits into the teachings of the end-times and rightfully so. We experience the kingdom here and now, but it is only in part. It has not yet been revealed in its fullness. That will happen on the last day, the Day of the Lord, spoken of in several New Testament letters[3]. On that day Christ our Savior will return to finish the job he started on the cross. He will return to save us and pronounce judgment; this will be the final expression of God's kingdom upon the earth.

So right now what we have before us is a partial fulfillment of his kingdom. It is expressed in the slogan of many present-day

---

2. Saint Augustine, *Confessions*, 8:7.

3. 1 Thess 4:13–18; 2 Thess 2:1–12; 1 Tim 6:14–15.

theologians as being *already, but not yet,* or as I prefer, *it is both here and yet to come.*[4]

> *"Therefore stay alert, because you do not know on what day your Lord will come. But understand this: If the owner of the house had known at what time of night the thief was coming, he would have been alert and would not have let his house be broken into. Therefore you also must be ready, because the Son of Man will come at an hour when you do not expect him. (Matthew 24:42–44 NET)*

In this small parable Jesus warns us to always be ready for his return—the Day of the Lord. Not that we should try to figure out the day and hour as many have unsuccessfully done, but to anticipate the kingdom's arrival so that we might be prepared at this very moment. Our obligation is to always be prepared for his coming since we don't know when it will be.

The preparation day for the kingdom's coming is always today. So we must not take this world too seriously and cling to it too closely because it is even now already passing away:

> *And the world is passing away with all its desires, but the person who does the will of God remains forever. (1 John 2:17 NET)*

---

4. Blomberg, *Jesus and the Gospels,* 384; Fee, *The First Epistle,* 173.

DISCUSSION QUESTIONS

1. Does your faith give you a sense of power over sin and this world?

2. Does Paul's advice in the quotation from Romans 12 seem a little extreme for an everyday churchgoer?

3. Have you ever been guilty of praying to God with the same attitude of Augustine? (Be honest)

4. What does it mean to be double-minded?

5. Do you think that too many churches focus upon the "Coming of Christ" as a final event rather than as an ongoing process?

6. Explain the meaning of the phrase, "Already, but not yet."

7. Is the kingdom here for you now? If not, what are you doing about it?

NOTES

Matthew 7:13–14 (NET)

"Enter through the narrow gate, because the gate is wide and the way is spacious that leads to destruction, and there are many who enter through it. But the gate is narrow and the way is difficult that leads to life, and there are few who find it."

5

How Do We Get into the Kingdom?

So how do we get into this kingdom? Do we simply repeat some words on a prayer card or enter in through the performance of some ritual? Must we first complete so many hours of door to door evangelism to qualify, or do we just have to make sure that we join the correct church? This brings up the underlying question, "Is the church the same thing as the kingdom of heaven?" I will answer this question in a later chapter.

Entry into the kingdom is in some ways easier than getting accepted into a church, but in some ways it can also be much harder.

Jesus tells us that many seek, but few will find. Many enter in through the wide gate and spacious way that leads to hell, but we must enter by the narrow gate, which is the difficult way, and only a few will find it.[1]

Now it certainly makes sense that it would be easier to find and enter through a gate that's large and has a spacious path, but not so easy to find and enter through the gate that is narrow where entry is difficult.

We must be careful, however, not to try to interpret too much detail into Jesus' advice since it's obviously metaphorical. The basic

1. Matt 7:13–14.

idea of his warning is that what might appear easier and less de-manding may very well lead to disastrous results. And what might appear to be more restrictive and difficult can lead to something much more rewarding. It intimates that the more committed we are to finding the kingdom the more willing we are to continue through difficulties until we find it. Are we looking for the true path into the kingdom or simply taking the path of least resistance? This parable is both asking us and warning us to decide just how much we are willing to struggle in order to gain entry.

This metaphor seems to be in direct conflict to the ease at which many today think they can enter into the kingdom of heav-en, but we need only reflect upon the demands that Jesus made upon his followers in his Sermon on the Mount to support this teaching about the difficulty of entering his kingdom. There will be many sacrifices one will have to make in this world if one decides to seek after God's kingdom. Jesus' own life was evidence of this as well as that of Peter, Paul and the other apostles.

It is much easier to take the road traveled by the majority and simply follow the crowd. Today we call this way the politically cor-rect road. To find the kingdom of God and walk in it requires that we leave the easy, well-traveled road and be willing to take the risks that go with taking the more difficult one—the one less traveled.

The narrow gate is difficult to find because many are simply looking in the wrong place for it. Instead of looking towards God they are looking inward towards themselves. They are seeking the kingdom through their philosophies and new-age ideologies. They see the righteousness of God in Christ and quickly look away be-cause it is just too bright and blinding for their eyes. They prefer to remain in the crowd where it appears dark and safe and much easier upon their eyes.

> And this is the condemnation, that light is come into the
> world, and men loved darkness rather than light, because
> their deeds were evil. (John 3:19 KJV)

Another meaning that emerges here is that the true gate is difficult to find and enter because it is so very much against our nature. It's not that we don't want to enter, but rather that we want to enter on our own terms. The way is difficult not because it's complicated, but because we resist God's will at every step. It simply demands that we admit to our helplessness when it comes to being righteous—and I think we can all agree that is no easy task. It is this self-denial that holds many back from entry into the kingdom.

> *Then said Jesus unto his disciples, If any man will come after me, let him deny himself, and take up his cross, and follow me. (Matt 16:24 KJV)*

Many see the narrow gate and may even walk upon the path leading to it, but they stop short of actually entering in. These are the ones who are unwilling to make a commitment of faith. They may love to hear the choir sing songs about God and might even be moved to tears by the pastor's sermon, yet they make no further move closer to the gate. They are content with the view they have. Perhaps they realize that once they make this move they will see themselves in a whole new light that will require changes in their life. Or perhaps they fear what others, including God, might see in their hearts, and that they will no longer be able to maintain their integrity and prestige that has taken them a lifetime to create. But unless one actually walks through the gate he cannot enter into God's kingdom.

As opposed to the Pharisees, Jesus' way of seeking God requires the loss of oneself rather than the adornment of oneself; and unlike many new-age ideologies, finding the kingdom of heaven is not self-discovery, but self-abandonment. It is through the spirit of sacrifice rather than achievement that enables us to draw nearer to God, which is what was originally preached in the Reformation. However, we must also understand that no matter how diligently we seek the kingdom and how much we sacrifice for it, we cannot find it under our own power.

The bottom line is that we must seek the kingdom of heaven with all our heart in response to his calling and offer ourselves as living sacrifices in response to his choosing us.[2]

Before I end this chapter I must mention that the narrow gate of which Jesus is speaking is not the mythical gate portrayed in movies and on TV. Jesus is not speaking about some pearly gate guarded by Saint Peter who checks to see if our name is on the entry list. If our good deeds outweigh our bad deeds Saint Peter gives us entry, but if our bad deeds outweigh our good deeds we are sent away to another place not quite as nice.

Unfortunately, the cinema has had a great impact upon not only the world's idea of heaven, but also upon the church's. Far too many church members have a similar idea of heaven based upon this model rather than the biblical one given by Jesus. I will speak more about the church in a later chapter.

2. See Rom 12:1.

DISCUSSION QUESTIONS

1. Give examples of other ways people are told that they can enter into the kingdom of heaven.

2. Has the modern church preserved Jesus' teaching about the gate being narrow and the way difficult that leads to the kingdom? Why or why not?

3. Does the Sermon on the Mount support Jesus' teaching about the kingdom or contradict it?

4. What makes the gate so hard to find and the path so difficult to walk today?

5. Do you agree with the author that many are simply looking in the wrong place for the kingdom? Why?

6. What does the author mean by the difference between self-discovery and self-abandonment?

7. How do you think we can get into the kingdom of heaven?

NOTES

Matthew 7:21 (NET)

"Not everyone who says to me, 'Lord, Lord,' will enter into the kingdom of heaven — only the one who does the will of my Father in heaven."

6

Who Can Get into the Kingdom?

IT SEEMS THAT SOMETIMES Jesus spent more time warning us about all those who *can't* get into his kingdom than those who *can*. Some of his parables teach us that those who are excluded from his kingdom were excluded because they placed too high of an importance upon themselves and their ambitions. This self-importance led to self-deception which then became the basis of their false understanding. But not only did they deceive themselves; they deceived others as well. They deceived themselves by thinking that based upon their distorted system of values they deserved the kingdom. And they deceived others by teaching their deceptions as true knowledge based upon the false authority of men, not God. The truth is that no one deserves the kingdom—it is a gift of God.

It might be of interest to mention that according to scripture deception was not the *cause* of their error, but actually the *result* of it.

> And with all deceivableness of unrighteousness in them
> that perish; because they received not the love of the truth,
> that they might be saved. And for this cause God shall send
> them strong delusion, that they should believe a lie: That

> *they all might be damned who believed not the truth, but*
> *had pleasure in unrighteousness. (2 Thess 2:10–12 KJV)*

The deception took place because they rejected what was true and were pleased with themselves for doing so.

If we read Jesus' words in Matthew's record of the Sermon on the Mount we can see that Jesus lays out very strict guidelines for those who want to follow him. The criteria that he sets is that those who wish to be his disciples must be willing to make God their lord. Now this does not mean that we should turn God into some kind of political figurehead who lets us do whatever we want in the name of freedom, but one who by the very nature of his being is righteous and therefore calls upon us to also be righteous.

> *Like obedient children, do not comply with the evil urges*
> *you used to follow in your ignorance, but, like the Holy*
> *One who called you, become holy yourselves in all of your*
> *conduct, for it is written, "You shall be holy, because I am*
> *holy. (1 Peter 1:14–16 NET)*

In Matthew Jesus clearly tells us that it's not those who simply call him lord that will enter his kingdom, but those who actually demonstrate that God really is their lord who will enter.

> *"Not everyone who says to me, 'Lord, Lord,' will enter into*
> *the kingdom of heaven — only the one who does the will of*
> *my Father in heaven." (Matt 7:21 NET)*

Now it's not a very popular theme today, but Jesus gave us numerous parables making it very clear that there are some who will be excluded from his kingdom and thrown into darkness. In one such parable a king threw a grand wedding banquet for his son and invited all the important people in the town to come. After they refused to come and even beat up his servants, the king sent armies to destroy them. Then he invited all those who were considered to be the least worthy to come to the feast. But one of them decided he wasn't going to show respect to the king and his son by wearing the special wedding garment that was socially appropriate for him to wear to the wedding. When the king saw this he was enraged and had him thrown out of the feast.[1]

So even though many are called by God to enter, one must not confuse being called with being chosen. We must always maintain respect for God by seeking to perform whatever he might ask of us no matter how secure we might feel about our salvation (Matthew 22:2–14). As it was for this unfortunate man at the wedding it is for anyone who demonstrates by their behavior that they don't belong in his kingdom—they too will be excluded into outer darkness.

There are many more parables that Jesus spoke concerning this issue, but if you get the general idea presented here, you should be able to apply it to many of the other parables on your own.

The exclusion of some or even many doesn't mean that we should overlook the idea that all sinners certainly have the potential to get into the kingdom; otherwise, it would be a very lonely place for Jesus. As a matter of fact, Jesus tells us that sinners will go in even before the Pharisees. By this he doesn't mean that we ought to keep sinning to guarantee entry, but that those who know they are sinners and undeserving of the kingdom are in a better position and more likely to enter because they understand their need for repentance. It is for this very reason that we enter into the kingdom—so that God will help us to *stop* sinning and to *live* the life that Christ wants us to live.

So when Paul writes in 1 Corinthians 6:9–11 about those who are content in their self-deception and take pleasure in their sin, he is not writing about those who are believing members of the body of Christ (the church), but those who do not believe and are unrepentant for their sinful acts.

In 1 Corinthians 13:13 Paul tells us that God gave us three abilities through which we are to continue patiently: faith, hope, and love. Through these three we are to seek God's righteousness. We must first of all *love* God's righteousness. Second, we must *hope* that we will be able to demonstrate his righteousness to others. And lastly, we must fully have *faith* that this can and will be accomplished. Christ's righteousness is not optional. It must become part

---

1. Morris, *The Gospel According to Matthew*, 551.

of who we are. When we receive communion we must realize that to partake of Christ's body is also to partake of his righteousness. With the same enthusiasm that we eat of the body of Christ in the hope of obtaining salvation, we must also eat with the hope of obtaining his righteousness.

DISCUSSION QUESTIONS

1. What is self-deception and why is it so fatal to the truth?

2. What is your first reaction to 2 Thessalonians 2:10?

3. If we want to be righteous because God is righteous, won't we fall into the same deception of the Pharisees?

4. Do you think that God will really throw some people into outer darkness even after he invited them to become believers?

5. How do we demonstrate that we belong in the kingdom?

6. What's the difference between being called and being chosen?

7. Did you become a Christian just to be forgiven for your sins, or to stop committing them, or both?

8. How important was it for Christ to be righteous and why?

9. Do you agree with the author's last sentence of this chapter?

NOTES

John 6:66–68 (KJV)

From that time many of his disciples went back, and walked no more with him.
Then said Jesus unto the twelve, Will ye also go away?
Then Simon Peter answered him, Lord, to whom shall we go? thou hast the words of eternal life.

7

Why Should We Seek the Kingdom?

ONE OF THE PROBLEMS with the church today is that many are led to believe that once they're saved or become a member of the church that their search is over. Now their names are written in the *Book of Life* and that chapter is closed. Since no one tells them anything different they feel this is all that God has to offer them; so they live out their lives in a kind of grey area in regards to truth. Sure they might think that there's room for some clarity on a few doctrines like the Trinity and the Holy Spirit and for some improvement in regards to the sin in their lives, but for the most part their search for the kingdom is over.

The truth is that there is more to their Christian life than they realize. Salvation is only the beginning of their journey—not the end. If they would only search through the scriptures they would see that their search is far from over. The kingdom of heaven takes us well beyond the initial experience of salvation. Salvation is most certainly included in the kingdom, but one should never stop seeking the kingdom. When we seek the kingdom of heaven we

experience our state of salvation more deeply and grow to appreci-
ate it more passionately. Salvation is the beginning of a process that
must be worked out daily. Listen to what Paul tells the Philippians
about salvation:

> [W]ork out your own salvation with fear and trembling.
> For it is God which worketh in you both to will and to do
> of his good pleasure. (Phil 2:12–13 KJV)

Now the idea of the Christian journey needs a little explanation. The journey taken by the Christian is different than that
taken by other religions. It is not one of *searching for* the truth,
but one of *pursuing after* the truth. The Christian believes that he
has already found the truth, or rather the source of truth, which
is Jesus Christ. He is now committed to seeking after this truth,
not as something unknown and abstract, but rather in the absolute
form of the Kingdom of God.[1] Such a pursuit is a lifelong journey
committed to understanding oneself in a relationship of truth with
God. Each day he walks towards Christ guided by his faith and
motivated by his hope, drawn by the eternal truth of which he now
may only know in part, but will someday fully know face to face.[2]

Why then should we seek the kingdom? I doubt if anyone
has ever taken a survey of why people decide they want to enter
into the kingdom of heaven, but I would imagine one of the most
popular reasons would be because they have considered the alternative—hell. If we have a choice between choosing either heaven
or hell, I would assume most would choose heaven. But if one does
not believe in hell, then perhaps they see no good reason to choose
heaven or make any choice at all.

Jesus spent a lot of time teaching and warning those around
him about hell, and I can understand how hell could be a good
negative motivation to drive someone to choose heaven, but we
need to look a little deeper.

---

1. If you are interested in reading more on this subject, read either *The
Present Age* or *Fear and Trembling* by Soren Kierkegaard. *The Present Age* is a
far easier place to begin a study of Kierkegaard.

2. 1 Cor 13:12.

Many of us have probably come to our faith in Christ differently. Some come through beautiful preaching, while others through special events in their lives. Some have come to believe while sitting in a church and others while sitting in the park. So I can certainly see that some may have come to believe when confronted with a choice between heaven and hell and that choosing heaven therefore makes perfect sense.

But my point is that there's much more that heaven has to offer than simply being a better alternative to hell. The longer we seek after heaven and the more passionate our search becomes, the more we become drawn by its own inherent attractiveness. We begin to see it not as an alternative to hell, but to see it in its own light as God's kingdom of righteousness and holiness.

We begin to realize that this is the very reason that God created us. Man is not just a static creature of flesh and blood, but a dynamic one filled with spiritual curiosity. The kingdom of heaven is a state where we can achieve our full potential as spiritual beings. The kingdom of heaven opens to us a world of vision and hope that fulfills the desires of our innermost fabric of being. We are creatures of *being* and seek after a world that both fills and fulfills our need to *be* as well as to *become*. In other words, we are designed to live out our lives to their fullest potential.

A mistake that many make is that they think the kingdom of heaven is something distinct from God—it is not. We cannot seek heaven as something apart from the Lord, for the kingdom is defined by the very relationship created when he becomes both our Lord and our King. It is, therefore, imperative that we think about the kingdom of heaven in such terms of relationship rather than something distinct and apart from him.

There are also some who seek God's kingdom because they anticipate receiving a great reward. But Jesus warned about such an expectation. The parable of the vineyard laborers teaches directly to this issue.[3]

The parable teaches that those laborers who were hired first spent the most time working in the field and therefore, expected

3. Matt 20:1–16.

more pay than those who were hired later. Even though they were initially satisfied with the wages promised them for their work, they became angered because those hired after them were paid the exact same wage.

The underlying lesson is that rewards are subject to the value we create for them. Anticipating a reward may in fact diminish our sense of its value. So it is best not to work anticipating a reward, but to accept whatever the Master gives to us as a generous and undeserved wage.

There is another reason why some may want to get into heaven which is both understandable and sympathetic. It is to be re-united with lost loved ones.

Although I can sympathize with this sad situation, I must repeat what I said earlier that the kingdom cannot be separated from God and his holiness. We may be motivated by the desire to be reunited with a loved one, but we cannot simply decide to go to heaven. It is our re-union with God that must be of utmost importance, regardless of how much we want to be re-united with a loved one.

Many are under the impression that we simply decide to go to heaven and that's all there is to it. The problem with this is that heaven is a relationship with God that can only happen when God calls us. What this means is that by God's grace he makes us aware of his love as well as his righteousness. Our decision is a reaction to his presence not the cause of it; otherwise, we would be in danger of creating our own god on our own terms and simply deceiving ourselves.

Sometimes a major event in our lives can make us painfully aware of the realities of this life which can make us crave something beyond it. These events can affect us by causing us to re-evaluate our lives and for the first time begin to listen for the voice of God. Remember that prayer is not always speaking to God; sometimes it's simply learning how to listen.

Perhaps one of the most dramatic and passionate experiences we can have in his kingdom is simply knowing that God knows us.[4] Not only does he know us but he loves us enough to save us. What a horrible thought it is to think that the Power that created the universe either doesn't or simply can't know us on a personal level—that it can't even know that we exist! Within a few years after our death we will simply be forgotten and eventually our memory will disappear forever.

> But he that entereth in by the door is the shepherd of the sheep. To him the porter openeth; and the sheep hear his voice: and he calleth his own sheep by name, and leadeth them out. And when he putteth forth his own sheep, he goeth before them, and the sheep follow him: for they know his voice. (John 10:2–4 KJV)

But God, through Christ, not only remembers us, he saves us and creates a place for us in eternity. He will even remember our name for eternity.[5] This is what we need to be preaching today about God's kingdom to a hopeless world in despair.

In our new kingdom relationship with God, we can come to know him not only as servants, but also as sons and daughters. Since we exist as both spiritual and physical beings we are able to know God through both a physical relationship as servants and a spiritual one as his sons and daughters.

And finally the kingdom of heaven gives us a view into the eternal wonders and mysteries of God. While in the kingdom of heaven we can see not only the vastness of his eternal wonders, but the depths of eternal mysteries. Such mysteries and wonders can now be penetrated with the hope and expectation of being more fully understood and experienced as we grow to maturity in this kingdom.

4. 1 Cor 8:3.

5. Revelation 3:5, 21:27.

DISCUSSION QUESTIONS

1. Is your salvation complete or continuing towards completion?

2. Did you get the idea that Paul thought of himself as a finished work of God or still under construction?

3. Do you believe in hell? Do you admit it publically or are you embarrassed to admit it?

4. Do you think Jesus believed in hell based upon his teachings?

5. Do you have a relationship with God? How would you describe it?

6. Which is a more intense experience: the receiving of a gift or the anticipation of receiving it? How does your answer relate to the parable of the vineyard laborers?

7. Does it comfort you to know that God knows your name and has prepared a place for you?

NOTES

Matthew 5:17–18 (KJV)

Think not that I am come to destroy the law, or the prophets: I am not come to destroy, but to fulfil. For verily I say unto you, Till heaven and earth pass, one jot or one tittle shall in no wise pass from the law, till all be fulfilled.

8

The Kingdom and the Law

ONE OF THE MOST difficult issues that I faced throughout my own Christian journey is the relationship between the kingdom of heaven and the law of God. Both Jesus and Paul made statements about the law and how it was to be used, but I was still unable to put everything together to determine exactly the role of the law and how it related to my faith in the kingdom.

At first it appeared simple. We are no longer under the law, but under grace. Yet when we look around as to how this is applied by the churches, we see many different degrees of adherence under the law as well as different degrees of freedom under grace.

Does being under grace mean that the law is no longer valid for the Christian and there is no longer any legal restrictions against murder, adultery, or stealing? But, on the other hand, if we consider these as acts of sin, are we not then still under the law and obligated to keep it in its entirety? This kind of thinking created within me a conflict that had no easy resolution.

Apparently, I was not the only one who had a problem as to where to place the value of the law in a gospel of grace. The book

Five Views on Law and Gospel will be an eye-opener for those who think this issue is clear within all the Christian denominations and their respective theologians.[1]

What is even more surprising is that even during the time of Paul there was a lot of confusion in the church on the issues of law and grace. We get the idea from Paul's letters that there was perhaps more than a little tension between Paul's idea of grace and those who were presumed to represent the Jewish Christians from the church in Jerusalem. Exactly where James and Peter stood is difficult to say, and we must also understand that Christian maturity is an ongoing process even among those presumed to be pillars of the church.

This may have been the most threatening problem that the church encountered in its early formation, and it is still a problem that continues today to create tension and discontinuity within the modern-day church. But before we get too involved in the application of the law we must first clarify what we mean by law.

This is not a very easy question to answer since the meaning of the word law can vary greatly depending upon the context of the author. It could range anywhere from referring to the Ten Commandments to referring to the entire contents of first five books of the Bible written by Moses (Genesis–Deuteronomy).[2]

Many times in the New Testament the term law is best understood to include all the legal requirements that were established through the temple system. This would include the sacrifices, purification rites, and the priesthood to mention a few. It appeared to develop into a somewhat generic term for life under the legalities of the Old Covenant, but during the time of Christ the idea of law was comingled with rules and regulations established by men such as the Pharisees who tried to clarify the law by adding to it.

Some theologians divide the law into categories of moral, ceremonial, and civil law.[3] Please do not consider these as exclusive categories of law as though each aspect of law had to neatly

---

1. See the Bibliography for details on this book.
2. Bahnsen, Law and Gospel, 305.
3. Ibid., 30.

fit into either one or the other. These are just viewpoints of law depending upon the context of the scripture and the purpose the author wanted to express. I will try to make it clear throughout this chapter which meaning best fits my context, but it is best to take it in the most general sense unless otherwise directed.

The purpose of the law, as we see in the writings of Paul to the church at Rome, was to reveal man's sinfulness.[4] We get the idea that here Paul is referring more to the actual commandments of God, but this is not always his exclusive use of law. We also find that the book of Hebrews refers to the purpose of the law in a more prophetic manner, pointing forward to the Messiah and the redemption that would eventually take place as the new kingdom became established. For this author the law was a shadow of the wonderful things to come under the rule of the new and eternal king of Israel—Jesus.

So even though the law may best be known as having a moral and ethical purpose, we must not forget that it also had a prophetic purpose pointing to the Messiah as I will later show.

The gospels offer us some insight into what Jesus himself thought of the law. They tell us that several times he was confronted by the Pharisees with questions on the law, but his answers often seemed ambiguous and opaque and by themselves didn't fully clear up this mystery.

One time Jesus was confronted by the Pharisees because his disciples were breaking off heads of grain on the Sabbath. Many considered this to be a violation of Moses' law against working on the Sabbath. Jesus answered them by declaring that since the priests worked in the temple on the Sabbath it was legal for his disciples to do the same. His justification for this was that someone greater than the temple was here. I'm sure that Jesus' answer did little to satisfy the accusing minds of the Pharisees.[5]

From Jesus' answer, however, we can now see that he thought the purpose his ministry had priority over that of the whole temple system of Moses. It was in this sense that the temple system itself

4. Rom 7:7.

5. Matt 12:6.

was pointing to the very one who stood before them, but this would not have its full significance until after his resurrection.

In one of Jesus' most profound statements he tells us that his mission was not to destroy the law, but to *fulfil* it.[6] No one since the law was established ever claimed such an audacious role for himself and certainly no one since. From this comment we can deduce that Jesus believed that up until that time all men stood in a state of un-fulfillment under the law. This meant that under the old covenant such a fulfillment had not yet reached completion—but all that was soon about to change.

The moral laws as found in the Ten Commandments and elsewhere not only set a standard of behavior for the Jews, but also gave a portrait of the ethics and morality of the future Messiah.

The real conflict between the kingdom and the law occurs when a believer decides to live under the law to one degree or another. By so doing he declares his failure to fully realize the coming of the Messiah and his fulfillment of the law.

It is a failure to properly understand how grace and law can co-exist in the kingdom. Such failure is a result of our false perception of law and grace as antagonists rather than complements.

In the kingdom of heaven we are no longer under the law in the sense that the law has already brought us to the state of repentance and can do no more. It has shown us the perfect righteousness that God expects from the perfect man and the failure of man to meet this standard. Such a state of understanding creates in man a sense of guilt and deep regret that expresses itself in the form of repentance. At this point man can only realize his true state of hopelessness (despair) in that he does not possess the power to forgive himself and bring about his own salvation. At this point and only at this point can man realize the *grace* of God by abandoning himself to his hope in the anticipation of God's mercy. And it is at this very moment that law flows into grace.

So our confession of guilt leads to repentance which creates in us a hope for mercy. Such hope is fulfilled through the cross of Christ where the hope of mercy becomes a reality. It is at this point

6. Matt 5:17.

that the prophetic quality of the law is complete. And it is at this point that our need for mercy is fulfilled.

It now becomes clear that our righteousness is not gained by imitating the perfect man through obedience of commandments and rituals; for this would never lead us to guilt, repentance, mercy, and grace producing true righteousness which comes through faith; but would only lead to a sense of arrogance and self-righteousness. True righteousness is not something that we acquire through strict regimen and fearful obedience to laws. It is the act of believing God and acting upon that belief in the form of faith.

Now one might say that if we are now free from the law and living by faith in the kingdom of God, we no longer need to worry about ethics or morality so we can do as we like with impunity. But this is under the assumption that God's love, mercy, and grace can be isolated from his other quality of righteousness. In Matthew, Jesus recited part of the Jewish prayer called *Shema Israel*:

> *Hear, O Israel; The Lord our God is one Lord: And thou shalt love the Lord thy God with all thy heart, and with all thy soul, and with all thy mind, and with all thy strength: this is the first commandment.* (Mark 12:29–30 KJV).

God is one, a unity, and we cannot separate God's love, mercy, or forgiveness from his righteousness. If we seek the love, mercy, and grace of God, we must also seek his righteousness since they are inseparable.

The point of this chapter is to show that the law had a purpose under the old covenant and still has a purpose today regarding the kingdom of heaven. It leads us to our sense of sinfulness as well as points us towards the Messiah. Both these elements of law were fulfilled in Christ so that the law would become complete and the new covenant could begin, which places us square in the midst of God's kingdom.

The final point is that although once we are in the kingdom we are no longer under the law, we are not free from a sense of God's righteousness. We must love and cherish his righteousness as much as we cherish his love, grace, and mercy. If we neglect to understand this unity of God, we have then become guilty of creating our own god in our own image for the sake of assuaging our own sinful conscience.

DISCUSSION QUESTIONS

1. Prior to reading this chapter how would you have defined the law?

2. After reading the chapter how would you now define the law?

3. Prior to reading this chapter how did the law fit into the practice of your faith?

4. Did you ever experience the sense of guilt from the law in the same way Paul experienced it? Explain.

5. How did Jesus relate to the law?

6. Are the law and grace antagonistic or complementary in the kingdom? Explain.

7. Is it easier for you to follow a list of rules or to live by faith? Explain.

8. After reading this chapter how would you respond to those who insist upon not eating pork or shellfish based upon the idea that they were considered unclean under the old covenant?

9. Many claim to be under the grace of God, but what are the signs of being under grace?

NOTES

1 Corinthians 1:18 (NET)

For the message about the cross is foolishness to those who are perishing, but to us who are being saved it is the power of God.

9

The Kingdom and the Cross

TODAY WE UNDERSTAND THE cross somewhat differently than they understood it in the first century. During that time it would not have been unusual to actually see people hanging on crosses outside the city or on the road leading into it. In approximately 71 BC the Romans crucified 6,000 rebels led by Spartacus, hanging them on crosses along the Appian Way.[1] Josephus tells of 500 Jews being crucified each day during the siege of Jerusalem and being hung before the walls of the city.[2] History contains many such stories of crucifixion during the period around the first-century AD.

It is not my intention to describe the event of crucifixion in detail here, but rather to help you to see it through the eyes of the first-century Gentile or Jew as a reality and the role it played in our salvation. The fear that such a sight must have created is beyond description. Time and culture sometimes cause us to lose touch with the historic reality that lies behind such a religious icon. Today we use it in our artwork and jewelry as well as place it in our homes and churches as reminders or symbols of our faith. Recently, some film-makers have tried to recapture the horror on

---

1. Appian, *Civil Wars*, 1.120.
2. Rogers, *The Topical Josephus*, 185.

the screen, but it still remains almost fictional for most of us since we have learned to separate the screen from reality.

My point here is to try to make a connection between this apparatus of death and the kingdom of God. For either a first-century Jew or Gentile to accept the fact that their king was hung on a cross and left to die such an ignominious death required more faith than we realize today. We sometimes need to be reminded of not just the horror of the crucifixion, but the stigma attached to it as well.

When Paul uses the term cross he uses it as a metonymy. This simply means that he uses the cross as an abbreviation for the entire event of the passion. For him the cross includes the actual crucifixion as well as the events surrounding it, including both the resurrection and the ascension. For Paul it symbolizes the entire act of God's salvation event.

None of the events that occurred during the crucifixion occurred by accident. Even though many were done in mockery, they all played an important role in the coronation of Jesus as king. It was the Roman soldiers who provided Jesus with a cloak for a robe, a reed for a scepter, and thorns for a crown, followed by his triumphant walk to receive his final moment of glory—the cross.[3] Even the accusation placed above his head declared him to be the king of the Jews.[4] Finally, when everything was in place and about to be fulfilled, Jesus announces with his last cry, "It is finished."[5]

Within this salvation act are so many facets of symbolic meaning that we simply can't address all of them in detail in this short book. They range from the payment and redemption for Adam's sin to the fulfillment of the sacrificial system that God instituted in the Jewish system of law.

It is through the horror of the cross that the moment of Jesus' lordship as king actually begins. And his first act as king is that of conquering death itself. By doing so he creates the entry point for us into his eternal kingdom through faith. This is the paradox

3. Matt 27:27–31.

4. Matt 27:37.

5. John 19:30.

of which Paul speaks of in 1 Corinthians—salvation through the cross.

> For the message about the cross is foolishness to those who are perishing, but to us who are being saved it is the power of God. (1 Cor 1:18 NET)

The cross is the entry point for us into the kingdom of heaven because it is at this point that our faith transcends all things on this earth. Up until this point in history faith was always placed upon God through those things that existed in our reality: temples, lambs, priests, and such things. But now the object of our faith opens up the world of eternity to us through belief in something higher than our physical reality: the Resurrection which came to us by means of the cross.

Without this belief our faith remains earth-bound, but with it we become heaven-bound. This is the very reason that God chose such an event to establish his kingdom. It is for the purpose of lifting man up out of *this* reality and into God's. As I wrote in an earlier chapter "he brought his kingdom upon us through his cross which pierced through our reality and into his, enabling man not only to seek after God's kingdom, but to actually enter into it for all eternity."

No other means of entry is possible because no other means can pierce through from our reality into God's. And why do our works fall short and amount to nothing in the light of such a salvation? Because all our works are also earth-bound and cannot break through into God's eternal reality. Regardless of how wonderful our works are or how much money we may give to charity, or whatever position of respect we rise to in the church, they all begin and end in our plane of existence. The only act of righteousness that transcends this plane is that of God's act of salvation through the cross.

> But may I never boast except in the cross of our Lord Jesus Christ, through which the world has been crucified to me, and I to the world. (Gal 6:14 NET)

As you can see, for Paul the cross was not optional to the church or believer. It would belie the very foundation of our salvation if we acted as though the cross were simply an optional accessory to our faith and had no more meaning than a cosmetic piece of jewelry.

We must remember that our salvation is not established by the death of Christ, but upon his resurrection. It is upon this claim that many may have doubts since we were raised on the idea of belief being based upon overwhelming or at least persuasive proof. Science certainly does make it difficult to believe in such a miraculous event. But this is not something that one believes based upon proof.

> For since in the wisdom of God the world by its wisdom did not know God, God was pleased to save those who believe by the foolishness of preaching. For Jews demand miraculous signs and Greeks ask for wisdom, but we preach about a crucified Christ, a stumbling block to Jews and foolishness to Gentiles. (1 Cor 1:21–23 NET)

Scripture makes it evident that God chose such an event to frustrate those who use worldly wisdom and those who seek after endless signs. The resurrection is a belief that arises from surrendering oneself to God. It is more a *sign* of a person's faith in God and a *result* of that faith rather than a *means* to accomplish it.

Some have tried to defend their lack of belief in the resurrection by restating or redefining it as merely the resurrection of Jesus' ideology or teachings, and that faith in the resurrection is not necessary as long as you believe that Jesus was a great man or even a prophet. But such an idea cannot in any manner be justified by any of the New Testament writings. If one chooses to believe in such ideas, he is believing in another gospel and not the one preached by Paul or any other apostle.

> As we said before, so say I now again, If any man preach any other gospel unto you than that ye have received, let him be accursed. (Galatians 1:9 KJV)

Hopefully, it is now clear to you that there are not two Christianities or gospels: one with the cross and one without, or one with the resurrection and one without. For without the cross Christ becomes a mere philosopher-prophet, but with it, or rather through it, he becomes the Savior of the world.

DISCUSSION QUESTIONS

1. Do you wear a cross or keep one in the house? If so, what do you think about when you look at it?

2. Make your best effort to describe the feelings that a first-century Jew or Gentile might have seeing someone impaled upon a cross.

3. What are the benefits and consequences of showing the crucifixion of Christ in all its brutal reality?

4. Does all this about the cross make you think any differently of Jesus' words in Matthew 16:24 (KJV):

   Then said Jesus unto his disciples, If any man will come after me, let him deny himself, and take up his cross, and follow me.

5. What exactly do you think the author means by earth-bound faith and heaven-bound faith, and how are they different?

6. Do you know any Christians who believe faith in the resurrection is optional? How would you now respond to them?

NOTES

Matthew 16:21–23 (NET)

From that time on Jesus began to show his disciples that he must go to Jerusalem and suffer many things at the hands of the elders, chief priests, and experts in the law, and be killed, and on the third day be raised. So Peter took him aside and began to rebuke him: "God forbid, Lord! This must not happen to you!" But he turned and said to Peter, "Get behind me, Satan! You are a stumbling block to me, because you are not setting your mind on God's interests, but on man's."

10

The Kingdom and the Church

Now BACK TO THE question of whether the church is the same thing as the kingdom of heaven.[1] The whole idea of a church has become quite distorted from what it was during the time of Paul. In his day the church was simply thought of as a reference to all believers.[2] Sometimes it referred to a local congregation of believers as in the church at Corinth or the church at Jerusalem, but the local congregation was not thought of as a church in and of itself. The church was a term that referred to all those who believed, not some building made of brick and mortar, nor was it anything along the lines of a denomination.

As a matter of fact, Paul was appalled at the idea that some were segregating themselves by aligning with either Peter, Paul, or Apollos.[3] For Paul there was only one faith and therefore, only one church that was made up of all those who believed Jesus to be the Christ and who were committed to living that faith.[4]

1. Refer to chapters 1, 2, 3, and 7 for a definition of the kingdom of heaven.

2. The Greek word for church is ekklesia (εκκλησια), which means *people with shared belief, community, congregation,* BDAG, page 303–4 (3a–c).

3. 1 Cor 1:12, 3:4.

4. Eph 4:5

So in the early days of Paul those who were members of the church would likely have also been considered as members in the kingdom of heaven as well. Since there was only one Lord, there would also be only one church and one kingdom.

Throughout the history of the church a gap between the church and the kingdom developed. Unfortunately, today this gap has even widened. This is not to say that in Paul's day the church was perfect, for Paul's own letters testify that it was not. But today we seem to have lost almost all continuity between the kingdom and the church so that we must answer, "No, they are not the same."

What this means is that being a member of a church neither includes nor excludes anyone from being in the kingdom. It only means that the two are not synonymous.[5] What I am saying is that membership in a church certainly does not insure citizenship in the kingdom of heaven.

Today this gap continues to expand. One cause of this expansion is that some churches are going in a different direction than the one that Jesus originally gave it. Peter in the opening Bible verse of this chapter followed his good intentions of protecting Jesus and found himself in direct conflict with him. The problem he had was that he saw the prophecy of Jesus' death from the point of view of his own preconceived ideas and concerns and was unable to see God's will unfolding right before his eyes. Instead of being an asset to Christ during those last days he became a stumbling block.[6]

Such is the condition of many churches today. They no longer see their role as preaching the gospel of the kingdom and salvation to the world through the resurrection of Christ. They see themselves as creating a social utopia where everyone can live their lives in peace and happiness regardless of religion or belief. For them this is the kingdom of heaven. Learning to accept all beliefs as true has become their new mantra and *Great Commission*[7].

---

5. Morris, *The Gospel According to Matthew*, 351.

6. Matt 16:21–23

7. Matt 28:18–20.

Other churches are in danger of being absorbed into the business models of today's big businesses, measuring their success in terms of profits and gross product.

In this culture we have an attitude that says we must achieve success at any price. This may work in the business world, but we cannot let it become the attitude of the church. We cannot measure our success as a church by the same measures used in the world of business. We must see our success as simply doing the will of God as both an individual and as a body of believers. Such a value is not easy to measure and many times we simply have to exercise our faith regardless of the accompanying signs.

We seem to forget that Jesus, himself, taught that the message of the kingdom is not for the many, but for the few.[8] To appeal to the many requires that the message be changed. But this we must not do. We must preach the message accurately, in truth, and simply live with the results. The numbers are up to God. Our rewards will not be based upon church financial profits or even size of membership, but upon what we did with what we had and how we did it.

> When I came to you, brothers and sisters, I did not come with superior eloquence or wisdom as I proclaimed the testimony of God. For I decided to be concerned about nothing among you except Jesus Christ, and him crucified. And I was with you in weakness and in fear and with much trembling. My conversation and my preaching were not with persuasive words of wisdom, but with a demonstration of the Spirit and of power, so that your faith would not be based on human wisdom but on the power of God. (1 Cor 2:1–5 NET)

People are not converted by our skill as an orator or debater, but by the grace of God. Although this is the very foundation of our Protestant heritage, we still somehow want to think that we have some control over another's salvation—we do not!

What we do have are the gifts of the Holy Spirit. They are all gifts given to preach the message of the kingdom to the world

---

8. Matt 7:13, 14.

in truth and accuracy both *in word and in deed*. It is through this understanding that the church must see itself in the world, and it is based upon this that it will be judged.[9] The purpose for such gifts is to improve the church as Paul explains to the Corinthians:

> *It is the same with you. Since you are eager for manifesta-*
> *tions of the Spirit, seek to abound in order to strengthen*
> *the church. So the gifts are given to the church so that it*
> *cannot only preach the word in holiness, but live the word*
> *in holiness as well. (1 Cor 14:12 NET)*

What is the end goal of the church? Listen to Paul as he sums up both his goal and that of every believer.

> *God wanted to make known to them the glorious riches of*
> *this mystery among the Gentiles, which is Christ in you,*
> *the hope of glory. We proclaim him by instructing and*
> *teaching all people with all wisdom so that we may pres-*
> *ent every person mature in Christ. Toward this goal I also*
> *labor, struggling according to his power that powerfully*
> *works in me. (Col 1:28 NET1)*

This must be the goal not only of the bishop and pastor of a church, but also the Bible teacher and anyone else who has authority over another.

Although a gap exists between the kingdom and the church, there is still definitely a relationship between them. The *kingdom* is really a description of our relationship with God under Christ and the *church* refers to the people who congregate in his name. Now in an ideal world the members of the church would consist of only those who had this "authentic" relationship with God, and it would consist of only those who were also in the kingdom. Such a perfect world has eluded us—and perhaps it always has and always will. But we cannot let this discourage us from our end goal.

How do we close this gap? We have to simply once again preach the kingdom message with the same passion of Christ and

---

9. See also Rom 12:6–8

Paul. We must preach it not only by speaking it, but by living it as well.

From our present point of view we simply cannot see either the perfect church or the perfect kingdom, but I have no doubt that God most certainly can. This will be revealed to all of us when the *perfect* comes, but for now we must be content with seeing dimly into that mirror.[10]

With all the distractions in our world today it is easy to see how both the individual and the church can lose sight of its ultimate goal and sometimes it simply needs to be reminded of its ultimate duty to God. As sincere and good-hearted as Peter was, Jesus had to scold him for his own sake as well as preventing him from interfering in God's mission. In the end Peter became a great believer and apostle. This is also my wish and hope for the church today.

10. 1 Cor 13:9–12.

DISCUSSION QUESTIONS

1. How would you define the term "church"?

2. Do you think that having different denominations has helped or hurt the mission of the church?

3. How do you think Paul would respond to the above question?

4. Explain how someone can be a member of a church yet not in the kingdom of God.

5. What do you think is the mission of the church today?

6. When do you think the church came the closest to fulfilling its mission? Explain when and why.

7. What is the most prominent feature of your church that attracts people? What should it be?

NOTES

Matthew 13:11 (KJV)

He answered and said unto them, Because it is given unto you to know the mysteries of the kingdom of heaven, but to them it is not given.

11

Summary and Final Thoughts

WHENEVER WE TEACH OR write about a specific topic it is sometimes necessary to isolate aspects of that subject for the sake of discussion and analysis. The problem with this technique is that we create an artificial environment for the subject under discussion and remove the dynamic relationship which makes up the natural whole. It is here in the summary that I try to reunite these isolated aspects into a more natural and dynamic viewpoint. But please keep in mind that any explanation I offer will still fall short of the actual experience of God's kingdom.

So where then is the kingdom? It is all around us. It is wherever the presence of God is. This is not some feeling of Nirvana or sense of personal well-being aroused by music or some other emotional stimulus, but a presence of righteous power and divine glory as was demonstrated by Christ in his healings and miracles.[1]

We must be very careful not to confuse human feelings with the kingdom. Feelings are wonderful witnesses to its presence, but are not themselves the kingdom. The kingdom is an expression of our relationship with God and is not limited to some geographical area such as a church or cathedral creating an artificial religious mood by surrounding us with tokens of our faith with beautiful

1. 1 Cor 4:20.

music playing in the background. The kingdom is the experience of standing before God in truth, not standing before tokens or imitations of Him no matter how religious or holy they may seem to be or make us feel.

We know when we have found the kingdom of heaven because it is like finding a treasure that is worth more than anything we currently have and is worth selling everything to purchase it— if that were even possible.[2] In other words, we are willing to give up all we have in order to gain the kingdom of heaven. It becomes our life's ultimate concern, and we then begin to live accordingly.[3]

I know that many potential believers are unwilling to commit themselves to the kingdom until they have solved all of its puzzling mysteries, but that can never happen because those mysteries are eternal and will never end. There will always be just one more mystery that needs to be solved before they can make that commitment. Many answers to these mysteries, however, can only be understood once one enters into the kingdom and not before.

The kingdom is not something that we must passively wait for after death. It begins here and now and lasts for eternity. It is not something that comes at a time we choose and at our command, but rather something called forth by God and at his good pleasure.

It is currently not yet experienced in its fullness by us, but will come into its fullness on the day of Christ's return. For this reason it is said to be *already, but not yet;* or *both here and yet to come.*

It is hard to imagine anyone knowingly choosing hell rather than heaven, yet the kingdom of heaven is not simply an alternative to hell. It is something that we must seek out not because of what it *is not* (eternal darkness), but because of what it *is* (God's eternal Presence). Fear may push us towards heaven, but cannot push us into it.

The paradoxical nature of the kingdom makes entering it both simple and difficult. It is simple because it means all we have to do is let ourselves respond to God's invitation or calling by loving him in return for loving us; but it is difficult because

2. See Matt chapter 13 for parabolic examples of this attitude.
3. Tillich, *The New Being,* 152.

such simplicity goes against our basic nature that drives us to be independent and accomplish salvation on our own. (Maybe with a *little* help from God).

My own experience has taught me that loving God is not always as easy as it might sound. Many love God, but they love other things more. So first we must re-evaluate our lives and reconsider all those things that have become more important than God—including our own self-worth. But if we are willing, God will teach us how to do that and work with us in his own good time and in his own way to bring us to this realization. This is part of the process of being *called*.

It is the nature of God's love and righteousness that not everyone will respond to his calling, but in spite of what you may have heard or been taught, no one will be excluded from God's kingdom unless they choose to be. Anyone can enter regardless of the sins they have committed. It makes no difference what sins we have committed as long as we see them as sin and confess them as such and desire to turn away from them. The only sin that can't be forgiven is the one denying Jesus as the Christ. Our belief in Christ is evidence that we recognize the work and character of God in salvation. If we reject Christ, we are also rejecting the salvation of God.[4]

By now you may be asking yourself exactly why you wanted to enter into such a kingdom and if it's worth all the changes that it will bring about as you enter it; so it might be natural to ask what your reward will be for giving up everything as did Peter.[5]

In order to understand the problem of rewards we must first understand that seeking the kingdom of heaven is not something that we initiate from our own human desire. This fallacy is at the root of many cults and heresies who try to stand in the place of God and promise something that they cannot deliver. They will promise you some special knowledge of God or promise you a future kingdom where you will reign over many others less worthy

4. See John 1:18; John 5:19; John 5:23; John 8:18; John 10:30; 1 John 2:22–23; 2 John 9.

5. Matt 19:27. Pay close attention to the parable following in 20:1.

than yourself. Or they may promise to bring you into a higher sense of understanding. But this is only at best, a fantasy, and at worst, a willful distortion of truth for the purpose of profit. This comes about when man's motivation is based upon a desire for rewards.

The lesson here is that we must wait for God to respond to our seeking and not react too quickly when men answer in his stead with promises of future rewards.

We must seek the kingdom of God because we see in it the same value that is embedded in God himself. Seeking the kingdom is not seeking the kingdom as a place separate and distinct from God, but rather we seek it as the very dwelling place of God. What gives heaven its very value *is* the presence of God. We must seek it because our underlying need is to be with God and to live in his presence. Our greatest reward in the kingdom then is simply being in the presence of God for eternity. Seeking the kingdom for any other reward will always fall short and leave us feeling cheated as in the parable of the field-workers.[6]

But how can man seek God in such a manner if he has no idea of who God is? The answer to this lies in understanding what it means to *seek* God. What we call seeking is actually being drawn towards God by his holy presence. God initiates our seeking by drawing us towards himself through revelation, and this revelation is experienced though the expression of his Christ. It is our love and desire to be with God as we see him in Christ that draws us Godward and into the living presence of God. We must simply let God be true and seek after that truth.

The conflict between the kingdom and the law arises when we fail to understand the purpose and meaning of the law as it stands beside grace. From the law we learn that we are not perfect beings, but sinners in need of redemption, and it is in the law that we find a future promise of such redemption. Through the sacrificial system we see a predictor of the Messiah who will offer the ultimate sacrifice for his people. Through the rituals of purification we see a sense of his purity of character. And through the symbol

6. Matt 20:1–16.

of the priesthood we see one who will perfectly represent us before God.

Through Jesus' own teaching we learn that he was the very fulfillment of the law. He claimed to be greater than the temple because he was the human embodiment of it and the one to whom the whole law pointed.

Grace is the quality of God that we experience when we realize we can do nothing to deserve salvation yet discover that God has already provided a savior for us in the form of Christian.

We can then see that the law and grace are not antagonistic, but complementary in that they work together in the kingdom. The law leads us to God's kingdom through the expression of God's righteousness and his grace draws us in through the expression of his love.

Since God is one (unity) we cannot separate God's love, mercy, or forgiveness from his righteousness. If we seek the mercy of God, we must also seek his righteousness since they are inseparable.

I mentioned earlier that for Paul the cross represented the entire salvation act of God; but today the tendency is to isolate the cross from the idea of salvation by giving it a more universally acceptable meaning. This meaning may come in the form of peace, the power of good over evil, or merely a good-luck charm. It is not unusual today to see it being used as a decorative tattoo or a piece of jewelry to accent the Gothic style of dress, or even worn by street gangs, who perhaps believe it gives them some mystical power.

Paul did not view the cross as a symbol of peace or good over evil, nor did he use it as a good-luck charm, but to him it was the very power of God's salvation taking place through one of man's most horrific forms of penalty. The power of the cross lies in this ironic paradox. If you remove either the irony or the paradox, you are left with only an icon that means whatever you want it to mean.

Perhaps it is too late to recover the initial meaning of the cross in our culture, but we must make sure that we, at the very least, maintain its meaning in our own personal faith.

In regard to the kingdom and the church, all believers make up the body of the church which is also referred to as the body of Christ.[7] The term church as it refers to the building where believers meet was foreign to those of the first century as was the idea of denominations. In order to overcome this development, we must begin to think of ourselves, once again, as the believing body of Christ united under one Lord in the kingdom of heaven. By so doing we can close the gap between church and kingdom at least in principle if not in practice. This can become accomplished by making the church the messenger of the gospel of salvation through the resurrection of Christ, which is its true ministry.

In the meantime, all those who believe Christ to be their Lord are already in the true church and have an eternal place in the kingdom of heaven.

7. Col 1:24.

DISCUSSION QUESTIONS

1. Where is the kingdom of heaven?

2. How do you know that you're in the kingdom?

3. What would you say to someone who wants to believe, but puts it off until he gets more answers?

4. Do we have to wait until we die to go to heaven?

5. Why don't we understand all the mysteries of the kingdom of heaven?

6. Explain how someone enters the kingdom.

7. Why do you want to enter the kingdom of heaven anyway?

8. What are the rewards waiting for us in heaven?

9. How do we begin seeking God?

10. What role does the law play in leading us to the kingdom?

NOTES

Matthew 22:37–40 (KJV)

Jesus said unto him, Thou shalt love the Lord thy God with all thy heart, and with all thy soul, and with all thy mind. This is the first and great commandment.

And the second is like unto it, Thou shalt love thy neighbour as thyself. On these two commandments hang all the law and the prophets.

12

Conclusion: Love God

ONE MIGHT SAY THAT the simple conclusion to all this is to just love God as Jesus taught. But just how did he teach us to love God?

Jesus taught us to love God with all of our heart, soul and mind, and love our neighbor as ourselves (Matthew 22:37). Today, many churchgoers, pastors, and theologians think that this was an exaggeration or an example of Jesus' hyperbolic teaching since no one could really love God with all their heart, soul, and mind; but that's exactly what Jesus expects from us.

Unless we seek to love him in just that way our love can never transcend man's limited ability to love. It is only when man's love reaches its limit that it can then transcend that limit by means of the gifts that God gave us to do so: faith and hope.[1]

So what Jesus is commanding us to do is to set no boundaries on our love for God. Yet many consistently deny God of this boundless love, excusing themselves by the limits set by their own lower nature. The conclusion then is to not allow those who have failed to enter into God's kingdom to set the same limits that will

---

1. G. Fee explains in his commentary *The First Epistle to the Corinthians*, page 649–651 that according to 1 Cor 13:13 faith and hope which are temporal are given to us to produce a love which is eternal.

deny us entry. Take Jesus at his word and love the Lord with all the power you have within you without restriction.

Of course, at first we may not know exactly how to do this, and we may experience many failures to which I can personally testify. But God will teach us all we need to know and do in order to exceed those human boundaries. At the very least we should begin by using what he has already given us: faith, hope, and love in whatever quantities and qualities we presently have, knowing that faith and hope will produce eternal love.

Jesus gave us a good teaching example of this in the parable he told about the servants and the talents in Matthew 25:15. In this parable a man gave his servants different amounts of talents or coins before he took a trip. The first was given five, the second was given two, and the third was given one. The first two servants traded with them and earned double their investment. The third servant buried them and did not earn anything.

When the master returned the first two servants were able to give him the original talents as well as the profit that they earned. The master was so pleased that he made them rulers over many things. But the last servant, who buried his talent, could only give him back the one talent. This angered his master who called him wicked and lazy, and he was then thrown into the outer darkness.

The lesson here is that God expects us to have an attitude of wanting to do what pleases our Lord. Our work is not an act of labor, but an act of love, and that which differentiates labor from love is our attitude. So we must set our hearts upon using whatever means we have to please God, or else we too might remain in darkness.

Now there's one more thing to notice about Jesus' commands to love. Notice the order in which he gives them. First, we are to love God—then, we are to love our neighbor. This is no accidental order, but a precedent Jesus sets absolutely. By loving God we establish a relationship with him whereby we become intimate with both his grace and his righteousness. Only then can we love our neighbor in the manner which God sets for us as a model of divine love.

If we try to love our neighbor first, we create a human model of love that we then try to apply to God. This diminishes our relationship with him and his divine love to the level of man's. The result of this reversal of order can be seen today in man's turning the eternal God and King into his casual friend and pal in a relationship of equality rather than one of divine respect of which God is worthy.

How much then should we love God in the kingdom of heaven? With *all* of our heart, *all* of our soul, and *all* of our mind. We may never know if we can reach that perfect love, but we can be certain that if we don't try, we will never succeed. So our journey into the kingdom must begin with our first step towards it—loving God.

DISCUSSION QUESTIONS

1. If you could love God with all of your heart, soul, and mind right now, would you? What holds you back?

2. How can you remove the limits of your love for God?

3. Much of what Jesus taught involves having the right attitude. What is your attitude towards pleasing God?

4. What's wrong with trying to love God by loving our neighbor?

5. What does loving God mean to you?

NOTES

Matthew 23:13 (KJV)

But woe unto you, scribes and Pharisees, hypocrites! for ye shut up the kingdom of heaven against men: for ye neither go in yourselves, neither suffer ye them that are entering to go in.

13

A New Beginning

So now that we know all this about the kingdom of heaven, what should our next move be?

Today, we need to rekindle an interest in the foundational teachings of Jesus concerning the kingdom of heaven. This does not mean that we must minimize the role of the cross and the resurrection in any way as some have done, but we must understand why there is a resurrection and how it becomes the very entrance into the kingdom. We must refocus those who have drifted away from the kingdom message back to the foundational teachings of Christ and the apostles. Then we can rebuild the church on a more solid ground eliminating the cosmetic imitations as well as the needless complexities that have disguised the kingdom as mere doctrine and fantasy. It is upon this kingdom message that the resurrection stands. This is the message that declares Jesus as the King and Lord over all. Without this message the crucifixion is little more than a political execution, but with it his resurrection declares Jesus as Lord over all the heavens and earth and establishes his kingdom forever.

So here is where I leave you for now. Hopefully, I have stirred up your interest in the message concerning the kingdom of heaven. I hope that I have awakened within you something that you have been putting off or ignoring only because you thought it outside the realm of what faith could offer you. Or perhaps you simply feared to look deeper into your faith for fear that you would find more doubt than belief. I hope that I have showed you that your belief in such a kingdom can not only be hoped for but realized here and now at this very moment. For the kingdom of heaven is the very message that Jesus came to preach—and it is truly in your midst.

> *But seek ye first the kingdom of God, and his righteousness; and all these things shall be added unto you. Take therefore no thought for the morrow: for the morrow shall take thought for the things of itself. Sufficient unto the day is the evil thereof. (Matt 6:33–34 KJV)*

NOTES

Recommended Reading
for Further Study

Boice, James Montgomery. *The Parables of Jesus*. Chicago: Moody, 1983.

Bruce, F.F. *The New Testament Documents: Are They Reliable*. Leicester, Grand Rapids: Eerdman, 1998.

Conner, Kevin. *Mystery Parables of the Kingdom*. Victoria, Australia: K J C Publications, 1996.

Curtis, Kenneth A., et.al. *The 100 Most Important Events in Christian History*. Grand Rapids: Revell, 1991.

Gobnzalez, Justo L. *Church History An Essential Guide*. Nashville: Abingdon, 1996.

Greenlee, Harold J. *Introduction to New Testament Textual Criticism*. Peabody, Mass: Hendrickson, 1995.

Inrig, Gary. *The Parables: Understanding What Jesus Meant*. Grand Rapids: Discovery House, 1991.

Jeremias, Joachim. *Rediscovering the Parables: A Landmark Work in New Testament Interpretation*. New York: Charles Scribner's Sons, 1966.

Jones, Timothy Paul. *Christian History Made Easy*. Torrance: Rose, 2005.

Sailhammer, John H. *How We Got the Bible*. Grand Rapids: Zondervan, 1998.

———. *The Books of the Bible*. Grand Rapids: Zondervan, 1998.

Verbrugge, Verlyn D. *Early Church History*. Grand Rapids: Zondervan, 1998.

Wenham, David. *The Parables of Jesus*. Downers Grove: Intervarsity (IVP), 1989.

Wright, N.T. *The Challenge of Jesus: Rediscovering Who Jesus Was and Is*. Downers Grove: IVP, 1999.

———. *The Last Word: Scripture and the Authority of god-Getting Beyond the Bible Wars*. New York: HarperOne, 2005.

Bibliography

Appian, *Civil Wars*, Translated by Horace White. Loeb Classical Library, 1913. http://penelope.uchicago.edu/Thayer/E/Roman/Texts/Appian/ Civil Wars/1*.html

Blomberg, Craig L. *Jesus and the Gospels: An Introduction and Survey*. Nashville: Broadman & Holman, 1997.

Bruce, F.F. *Paul Apostle of the Heart Set Free*, Grand Rapids: Eerdmans, 1977.

Conner, Kevin. *Mystery Parables of the Kingdom*. Victoria, Australia: K J C Publications, 1996.

Cranfield, C.E.B. *The Gospel According to St Mark*, New York: Cambridge University Press, 1959.

Danker, Frederick William, rev. and ed. *A Greek-English Lexicon of the New Testament and Other Early Christian Literature*, Chicago: University of Chicago Press, 3rd ed. 2000.

Fee, Gordon. *The First Epistle to the Corinthians*, Grand Rapids: Eerdmans, 1987.

Bahnsen, Greg, et al. *Five Views on Law and Gospel*, Grand Rapids: Zondervan, 1999.

Kierkegaard, Soren. *Fear and Trembling*. Translated by Walter Lowrie. Princeton: Princeton University Press, 1974.

———. *The Present Age*. Translated by Alexander Dru. New York: Harper & Row, 1962.

Kim, Seyoon. *The Son of Man, as the Son of God*, 1983. Reprint, Eugene, OR: Wipf & Stock, 2011.

Morris, Leon. *The Gospel According to Matthew*. Grand Rapids: Eerdmans, 1992.

Rogers, Cleon L. *The Topical Josephus: Historical Accounts that Shed Light on the Bible*, Grand Rapids: Zondervan, 1992.

Saint Augustine Confessions, Translated by E. B. Pusey http://www.gutenberg. org/files/3296/3296-h/3296-h.htm

Tillich, Paul. *The New Being*, Lincoln, NEB: University of Nebraska Press, 2005.

www.ingramcontent.com/pod-product-compliance
Lightning Source LLC
Chambersburg PA
CBHW070508090426
42735CB00012B/2693